HOW TO
SPOT A
FASCIST

HOW TO SPOT A FASCIST

UMBERTO ECO

TRANSLATED FROM THE ITALIAN BY
Richard Dixon and Alastair McEwen

Harvill *Secker*

LONDON

11

Harvill Secker, an imprint of Vintage,
20 Vauxhall Bridge Road,
London SW1V 2SA

Harvill Secker is part of the Penguin Random House group
of companies whose addresses can be found at
global.penguinrandomhouse.com

Penguin
Random House
UK

Copyright © Umberto Eco 1997, 2011
Copyright © La nave di Teseo editore 2019

English translation copyright © Richard Dixon 2012
English translation copyright © Alastair McEwen 2001, 2020

First published by Harvill Secker in 2020

'Ur-Fascism' first published in Great Britain in the collection
Five Moral Pieces by Secker & Warburg in 2001, first
published in Italy with the title *Cinque Scritti Morali* by
RCS Libri S.p.A in 1997

'Censorship and Silence' first published in Great Britain in the
collection *Inventing the Enemy* by Harvill Secker in 2012, first
published in Italy with the title *Costruire il nemico e altri
scritti occasionali* by Bompiani/RCS Libri S.p.A. in 2011

'We Are European' first published in Italy in 2019 by
La nave di Teseo with the title 'Un nuovo trattato di Nimega'
in the selection *Migrazioni e intolleranza*. The essay is taken
from a speech held in 2012 at the University of Nijmegen,
in Holland, seat of the first European peace treaty in 1678.

A CIP catalogue record for this book
is available from the British Library

penguin.co.uk/vintage

ISBN 9781787302662

Typeset in 11/15 pt Stempel Garamond
by Jouve UK, Milton Keynes
Printed and bound in Great Britain by Clays Ltd, Elcograf S.p.A.

Penguin Random House is committed to a sustainable future for
our business, our readers and our planet. This book is made
from Forest Stewardship Council® certified paper.

MIX
Paper | Supporting
responsible forestry
FSC® C018072

Contents

Ur-Fascism

In 1942, when I was ten, I won the first prize at the *Ludi Juveniles,* a compulsory open competition for all young Italian Fascists – that is to say, for all young Italians. I had written a virtuoso piece of rhetoric in response to the essay title 'Should We Die for the Glory of Mussolini and the Immortal Destiny of Italy?' My answer was in the affirmative. I was a smart kid.

Then in 1943 I discovered the meaning of the word 'freedom.' I shall tell that story at the end of this speech. At the time 'freedom' did not yet mean 'liberation.'

I spent two of my earliest years surrounded by SS, Fascists, and Resistance fighters all busily shooting at one another, and I learned how to dodge bullets. It wasn't bad training.

In April 1945 the partisans took Milan. Two days later they arrived in the little town where I lived. It was a joyous moment. The main square was crowded with people singing and waving flags, calling loudly for Mimo, the leader of the local Resistance movement. A former sergeant in the Carabinieri, Mimo had thrown his lot in with the followers of Badoglio and had lost a leg in one of the first clashes. He appeared on the balcony of the town hall, pale; with one hand, he tried to calm the crowd. I was waiting for him to begin his speech, given that my entire early childhood had been marked by Mussolini's great historic speeches, the most important parts of which we used to memorise at school. Silence. Mimo's voice was hoarse, you could hardly hear him. He said: 'Citizens, friends. After so many painful sacrifices . . . here we are. Glory to those who fell for freedom.' That was it. He went back inside. The crowd gave a shout, the partisans raised their weapons and fired into the air in festive mood. We kids rushed to collect the shell cases, precious collector's items, but I had also learned that freedom of speech means freedom from rhetoric.

Some days later I saw the first American soldiers. They were African-Americans. The first Yankee I met was a black man, Joseph, who introduced me to the wonders of Dick Tracy and L'il Abner. His comics were in colour and smelled good.

One of the officers (a Major or Captain Muddy) was billeted in a villa owned by the family of two of my classmates. It was a home away from home for me in that garden where some ladies were clustered around Captain Muddy, talking in sketchy French. Captain Muddy was a well-educated man and knew a little French. So my first image of the American liberators, after all those pale faces in black shirts, was that of a cultivated black man in a yellow green uniform saying: '*Oui, merci beaucoup, Madame, moi aussi j'aime le champagne ...*' Unfortunately there was no champagne, but Captain Muddy gave me my first chewing gum and I chewed it all day long. At night I would put the gum in a glass of water, to keep it fresh for the next day.

In May we heard that the war was over. Peace gave me a curious feeling. I had been told that permanent war was the normal condition for a young Italian. Over the following months I discovered that the Resistance was not a local phenomenon but a European one. I learned exciting new words like '*reseau*,' '*maquis*,' '*armée secrète*,' '*Rote Kapelle*,' and '*Warsaw ghetto*.' I saw the first photographs of the Holocaust, and I learned what this meant even before I learned the word. I realised what it was we had been liberated from.

Some people in Italy today wonder if the Resistance had any real military impact on the course of the war. For my generation the question is irrelevant: we immediately understood the moral and psychological significance of the Resistance. It was a source of pride to know that we Europeans had not waited for liberation passively. I think that for the young Americans who were paying their tribute of blood for our freedom it was not useless to know that behind the lines there were Europeans who were already paying their debt.

Some Italians now say that the legend of the Resistance is a Communist lie. True, the Communists did exploit the Resistance as if it were their own private property, given that they played a primary role in it; but I recall partisans who wore kerchiefs of different colours.

Glued to the radio, I would pass the nights – with the windows closed, the blackout made the tiny space around the radio the only halo of light – listening to the messages that Radio London broadcast to the partisans. They were at once cryptic and poetic ('The sun also rises,' 'The roses will bloom'), and most of them were 'messages for Franchi.' Someone whispered to me once that Franchi was the leader of one of the most powerful clandestine groups in North Italy, a man of legendary courage. Franchi became my hero. Franchi (whose real name was Edgardo Sogno) was a monarchist, such a fervent anti-Communist that after the war he joined an extreme right-wing group and was accused of having collaborated in a reactionary coup. But what does it matter? Sogno is still the dream of my childhood.[1] The Liberation was a common undertaking achieved by people of different colours.

Today in Italy some people say that the war of liberation was a tragic period of division, and that now we need national reconciliation. The memory of those terrible years ought to be repressed. But repression causes neurosis. While reconciliation means compassion and respect for all those who fought the war in good faith, forgiving does not mean forgetting. I can even admit that Eichmann believed sincerely in his mission, but I do not feel like saying: 'Okay, go back and do it again.' We are here to remember

---

[1] A play on words: in Italian, *sogno* means 'dream.'

what happened and to declare solemnly that 'they' must never do it again.

But who are 'they'?

If we think again of the totalitarian governments that dominated Europe before the Second World War, we can easily say that they are unlikely to return in the same form in different historic circumstances. Mussolini's Fascism was based on the idea of a charismatic leader, on corporativism, on the utopia of the 'fateful destiny of Rome,' on the imperialistic will to conquer new lands, on inflammatory nationalism, on the ideal of an entirely regimented nation of Blackshirts, on the rejection of parliamentary democracy, and on anti-Semitism. I admit that Alleanza Nazionale, which sprang from the Movimento Sociale Italiano, is certainly a right-wing party, but it has little to do with the old Fascism. Similarly, even though I am worried by the various pro-Nazi movements active here and there in Europe, Russia included, I don't think that Nazism, in its original form, is about to reappear as a movement involving an entire nation.

Nonetheless, even though political regimes can be overturned, and ideologies criticised and delegitimised, behind a regime and its ideology there is always a way of thinking and feeling, a series of cultural habits, a nebula of obscure instincts and unfathomable drives. Is there then another ghost wandering through Europe (not to mention other parts of the world)?

Ionesco once said that only words count and all the rest is idle chatter. Linguistic habits are often important symptoms of unspoken sentiments.

Allow me therefore to ask why not only the Resistance but the entire Second World War has been defined all over the world as a struggle against Fascism. If you reread Hemingway's *For Whom the Bell Tolls,* you will discover that Robert Jordan identifies his enemies with the Fascists even when he is thinking of the Spanish Falangists.

I yield the floor to Franklin Delano Roosevelt: 'The victory of the American people and their allies will be a victory against Fascism and the blind alley of despotism that it represents' (23 September 1944).

During the McCarthy period, Americans who had taken part in the Spanish Civil War were called 'premature anti-Fascists' – another way of saying that fighting Hitler in the forties was a moral duty for all good Americans, but fighting against Franco too soon, in the thirties, was suspect. Why was an expression like 'Fascist pig' used by American radicals even to indicate a policeman who did not approve of what they smoked? Why didn't they say: 'Caugolard pig,' 'Falangist pig,' 'Ustasha pig,' 'Quisling pig,' 'Ante Pavelić pig,' or 'Nazi pig'?

Mein Kampf is the complete manifesto of a political programme. Nazism had a theory of race and Aryanism, a precise notion of *entartete Kunst* ('degenerate art'), a philosophy of the will to power and of the *Übermensch*. Nazism was decidedly anti-Christian and neo-Pagan, just as Stalin's *Diamat* (the official version of Soviet Marxism) was clearly materialistic and atheist. If by totalitarian we mean a regime that subordinates all individual acts to the state and its ideology, then Nazism and Stalinism were totalitarian regimes.

Fascism was certainly a dictatorship, but it was not wholly totalitarian – not so much for its moderation as for the philosophical weakness of its ideology. Contrary to commonly held belief, Italian Fascism did not have a philosophy of its own. The article on Fascism signed by Mussolini for the *Enciclopedia Treccani* was written or fundamentally inspired by Giovanni Gentile, but it reflected a late-Hegelian notion of the 'ethical and absolute state' that Mussolini never completely realised. Mussolini had no philosophy: all he had was rhetoric. He started out as a militant atheist, only to sign the Concordat with the Church and to consort with the bishops who blessed the Fascist banners. In his early anticlerical years, according to a plausible story, he once asked God to strike him dead on the spot, to prove His existence. God evidently had other fish to fry at the time. In subsequent years, Mussolini always mentioned God in his speeches and was not above having himself called 'the man of Providence.'

It can be said that Italian Fascism was the first right-wing dictatorship to dominate a European country, and that all similar movements later found a sort of common archetype in Mussolini's regime. Italian Fascism was the first to create a military liturgy, a folklore, and even a style of dress – which enjoyed greater success abroad than Armani, Benetton, or Versace today. It was not until the thirties that Fascist movements sprang up in England, with Mosley, and in Latvia, Estonia, Lithuania, Poland, Hungary, Romania, Bulgaria, Greece, Yugoslavia, Spain, Portugal, Norway, and even South

America, not to mention Germany. It was Italian Fascism that convinced many European liberal leaders that the new regime was implementing interesting social reforms capable of providing a moderately revolutionary alternative to the Communist threat.

However, this historical precedence does not strike me as sufficient to explain why the word 'Fascism' has become a synecdoche, a denomination *pars pro toto* for different totalitarian movements. It is pointless to say that Fascism contained in itself all the elements of successive totalitarian movements, so to speak, 'in a quintessential state.' On the contrary, Fascism contained no quintessence, and not even a single essence. It was a fuzzy form of totalitarianism. It was not a monolithic ideology, but rather a collage of diverse political and philosophical ideas, a tangle of contradictions. Is it possible to conceive of a totalitarian movement that manages to reconcile monarchy and revolution, the royal army and Mussolini's private militia, the privileges granted the Church and a state education system that extolled violence, total control, and a free market? The Fascist Party came into being proclaiming a new revolutionary order, but it was financed by the most conservative landowners, who were expecting a counterrevolution. The republican Fascism of the early days endured for twenty years, proclaiming its loyalty to the royal family, allowing a 'Duce' to soldier on arm-in-arm with a 'king' to whom he also offered the title of emperor. But when in 1943 the king sacked Mussolini, the party resurfaced two months later, with the help of the Germans, under the flag of a 'social' republic, thus recycling its old revolutionary score, enhanced by a quasi-Jacobin streak.

There was only one Nazi architecture, and one Nazi art. If the architect of the Nazis was Albert Speer, there was no room for Mies van der Rohe. In the same way, under Stalin, if Lamarck was right, there was no room for Darwin. In contrast, there certainly were Fascist architects, but alongside their pseudo Coliseums there also rose new buildings inspired by the modern rationalism of Gropius.

The Fascists had no Zhdanov. In Italy there were two important art prizes: the Premio Cremona was controlled by an uncultivated and fanatical Fascist like Farinacci, who encouraged propagandistic art (I can remember pictures with titles like *Listening to the Duce's Speech on the Radio* and *Mental States Created by Fascism*);

and the Premio Bergamo, sponsored by a cultivated and reasonably tolerant Fascist like Bottai,
who protected art for art's sake, and the new
avant-garde art that had been banned in Germany
as corrupt and crypto-Communist, contrary to
Nibelungian kitsch, the only art allowed.

The Italian national poet was D'Annunzio,
a fop who in Germany or Russia would have
found himself in front of a firing squad. He was
elevated to the rank of bard to the regime for his
nationalism and cult of heroism – with the add-
ition of a strong dash of French decadence.

Let's take futurism. It ought to have been
considered an example of *entartete Kunst,* like
expressionism, cubism, and surrealism. But the
first Italian futurists were nationalists. For aes-
thetic reasons they backed Italy's entry into the
First World War; they celebrated speed, violence, and risk, and in a certain way these aspects
seemed close to the Fascist cult of youth. When
Fascism identified itself with Ancient Rome and
rediscovered rural traditions, Marinetti – who
said an automobile was more beautiful than the
Victory of Samothrace, and even wanted to do
away with moonlight – was named a member
of the Accademia d'Italia, a body that treated
moonlight with great respect.

Many of the future partisans and intellectuals of the Communist Party were educated by the GUF, the Fascist association of university students, which was intended to be the cradle of a new Fascist culture. These clubs became a sort of intellectual melting pot in which new ideas circulated without any real ideological control, not so much because party officials were tolerant, but because few of them possessed the intellectual equipment required to keep a check on the clubs.

In the course of those two decades, the poetry of the so-called hermetic school represented a reaction to the pompous style of the regime. These poets were allowed to elaborate their literary protest from inside the ivory tower. The sentiments of the hermetic poets were exactly the opposite of the Fascist cult of optimism and heroism. The regime tolerated this overt, albeit socially imperceptible dissent, because it did not pay sufficient attention to such obscure jargon.

Which does not mean that Italian Fascism was tolerant. Gramsci remained in prison until his death, Matteotti and the Rosselli brothers were murdered, the free press suppressed, the labour unions dismantled, and political dissidents confined to remote islands. Legislative power became a mere sham, and the executive branch of government (which controlled the judiciary, and the mass media too) enacted new laws directly. This body of new law included the race laws (Italy's formal endorsement of the Holocaust).

The inconsistent image I have described here was not due to tolerance: it was an example of political and ideological chaos. But it was 'orderly chaos,' organised confusion. Fascism was philosophically unsound, but on an emotional level it was firmly anchored to certain archetypes.

We have now come to the second part of my case. There was only one Nazism, and we cannot describe the ultra-Catholic Falangism of Franco as Nazism, given that Nazism is fundamentally pagan, polytheistic, and anti-Christian, otherwise it is not Nazism. On the other hand, you can play the Fascism game many ways, and the name of the game does not change. According to Wittgenstein, what happens with the notion of 'Fascism' is what happens with the notion of 'play.' A game can be competitive or otherwise, it can involve one or more people, it may require some particular skills or none, there may be money at stake or not. Games are a series of diverse activities that reveal only a few 'family resemblances.'

Let us suppose that there is a series of political groups. Group 1 is characterised by the aspects *abc*, group 2 by *bcd*, and so on. 2 is similar to 1 insofar as they have two aspects in common. 3 is similar to 2 and 4 is similar to 3 for the same reason. Note that 3 is also similar to 1 (they share the aspect c). The most curious case is that of 4, obviously similar to 3 and 2 but without any characteristic in common with 1. Nevertheless, because of the uninterrupted series of decreasing similarities between 1 and 4, there remains, by virtue of a sort of illusory transitiveness, a sense of kinship between 4 and 1.

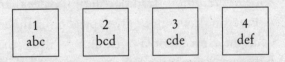

The term 'Fascism' fits everything because it is possible to eliminate one or more aspects from a Fascist regime and it will always be recognisably Fascist. Remove the imperialist dimension from Fascism, and you get Franco or Salazar; remove the colonialist dimension, and you get Balkan Fascism. Add to Italian Fascism a dash of radical anti-Capitalism (which never appealed to Mussolini), and you get Ezra Pound. Add the cult of Celtic mythology and the mysticism of the Grail (completely extraneous to official Fascism), and you get one of the most respected gurus of Fascism, Julius Evola.

Despite this confusion, I think it is possible to draw up a list of characteristics typical of what I should like to call 'Ur-Fascism,' or 'eternal Fascism.' These characteristics cannot be regimented into a system; many are mutually exclusive and are typical of other forms of despotism or fanaticism. But all you need is one of them to be present, and a Fascist nebula will begin to coagulate.

1. The first characteristic of Ur-Fascism is the *cult of tradition*. Traditionalism is older than Fascism. It was not only typical of Catholic counterrevolutionary thinking after the French Revolution but was born in the late Hellenic period as a reaction to classical Greek rationalism.

   In the Mediterranean basin, the peoples of different religions (all indulgently welcomed into the Roman pantheon) began dreaming of a revelation received at the dawn of human history. This revelation lay for a long time concealed under a veil of languages by now forgotten. It was guarded by Egyptian hieroglyphics, Celtic runes, and the sacred writings, still unknown, of the Asiatic religions.

This new culture was to be *syncretic*. 'Syncretism' is not merely, as the dictionaries say, the combination of different forms of beliefs or practices. A combination like this *must tolerate contradictions*. All the original messages contain a grain of wisdom, and when they seem to be saying different or incompatible things, it is only because they all allude, allegorically, to some original truth.

Consequently, *there can be no advancement of learning*. The truth has already been announced once and for all, and all we can do is continue interpreting its obscure message. It suffices to take a look at the syllabus of every Fascist movement, and you will find the principal traditionalist thinkers. Nazi gnosis fed on traditionalist, syncretic, and occult elements. The most important theorist of the new Italian right, Julius Evola, mixed the Grail with the Protocols of the Elders of Zion, and alchemy with the Holy Roman Empire. The very fact that, in order to demonstrate its open-minded stance, a part of the Italian right has recently widened its syllabus by putting together De Maistre, Guenon, and Gramsci is glaring evidence of syncretism.

If you browse through the New Age sections in American bookshops, you will even find Saint Augustine, who, as far as I know, was not a Fascist. But putting together Saint Augustine and Stonehenge, now *that* is a symptom of Ur-Fascism.

2. Traditionalism implies the rejection of modernism. Both the Fascists and the Nazis worshiped technology, while traditionalist thinkers usually reject technology as the negation of traditional spiritual values. Nevertheless, although Nazism was proud of its industrial successes, its praise of modernity was only the superficial aspect of an ideology based on 'blood and soil' (*Blut und Boden*). The rejection of the modern world was disguised as a condemnation of the capitalist way of life, but mainly concerned a rejection of the spirit of 1789 (or of 1776, obviously). The Enlightenment and the Age

of Reason were seen as the beginning of modern depravity. In this sense, Ur-Fascism can be defined as irrationalism.

3. Irrationalism also depends on the cult of *action for action's sake*. Action is beautiful in itself, and therefore must be implemented before any form of reflection. Thinking is a form of emasculation. Therefore *culture is suspect* insofar as it is identified with critical attitudes. From the statement attributed to Goebbels ('When I hear talk of culture, I take out my pistol') to the frequent use of expressions like 'goddamn intellectuals,' 'eggheads,' 'radical snobs,' 'The universities are a den of Communists,' suspicion of intellectual life has always been a symptom of Ur-Fascism. The official Fascist intellectuals were mainly committed to accusing modern culture and the liberal intelligentsia of having abandoned traditional values.

4. No form of syncretism can accept criticism. The critical spirit makes distinctions, and distinguishing is a sign of modernity. In modern culture, the scientific community

sees dissent as a tool with which to promote the advancement of learning. For Ur-Fascism, *dissent is betrayal*.

5. Dissent is moreover a sign of diversity. Ur-Fascism grows and seeks a consensus by exploiting and exacerbating the natural *fear of difference*. The first appeal of a Fascist or prematurely Fascist movement is a call against intruders. Ur-Fascism is therefore racist by definition.

6. Ur-Fascism springs from individual or social frustration, which explains why one of the characteristics typical of historic Fascist movements was *the appeal to the frustrated middle classes*, disquieted by some economic crisis or political humiliation, and frightened by social pressure from below. In our day, in which the old 'proletarians' are becoming petits bourgeois (and the lumpen proletariat has excluded itself from the political arena), Fascism will find its audience in this new majority.

7. To those with no social identity at all, Ur-Fascism says that their only privilege is the

most common privilege of all, that of being born in the same country. This is the origin of nationalism. Moreover, the only ones who can provide the nation with an identity are the enemy. Thus, at the root of Ur-Fascist psychology lies the *obsession with conspiracies*, preferably international ones. The disciples must feel that they are under siege. The easiest way to construct a conspiracy is to appeal to *xenophobia*. But conspiracies must also come from the inside: the Jews are usually the best target, because they offer the advantage of being at once both inside and outside. In America, the latest example of this obsession with conspiracies is Pat Robertson's book *The New World Order*.

8. The disciples must feel humiliated by the enemy's vaunted wealth and power. When I was a little boy, they taught me that the English were the 'five-meals people,' eating more often than the poor but sober Italians. The Jews are wealthy and help one another through a secret network of mutual assistance. But the disciples must nonetheless feel they can defeat the enemy. Thus, thanks

to a continual shifting of the rhetorical register, *the enemy is at once too strong and too weak*. Fascist regimes are doomed to lose their wars, because they are constitutionally incapable of making an objective assessment of the enemy's strength.

9. For Ur-Fascism there is no struggle for life but, rather, a 'life for struggle.' *Pacifism is therefore collusion with the enemy*; pacifism is bad, because *life is a permanent war*. This, however, brings with it an Armageddon complex: since the enemy can and must be defeated, there must be a last battle, after which the movement will rule the world. Such a *final solution* implies a subsequent era of peace, a Golden Age that contradicts the principle of permanent war. No Fascist leader has ever managed to resolve this contradiction.

10. Elitism is a typical aspect of all reactionary ideologies, insofar as it is basically aristocratic. In the course of history, all forms of aristocratic and militaristic elitism have implied *scorn for the weak*. Ur-Fascism cannot do without preaching a 'popular elitism.'

Every individual belongs to the best people in the world, party members are the best citizens, and every citizen can (or ought to) become a party member. But you cannot have patricians without plebeians. The leader, who is well aware that his power has not been obtained by delegation but was taken by force, also knows that his power is based on the weakness of the masses, who are so weak as to need and deserve a 'dominator.' Since the group is organised hierarchically (along military lines), each subordinate leader looks down on his inferiors, and each of his inferiors looks down in turn on his own underlings. All this looking down reinforces the sense of a mass elite.

11. From this point of view, everyone is trained to become a hero. In every mythology the hero is an exceptional being, but in the Ur-Fascist ideology heroism is the norm. This cult of heroism is closely connected to the *cult of death*: there is nothing accidental about the fact that the motto of the Falangists was '*Viva la muerte!*' Normal people are told that death is unpleasant but has to be faced with dignity; believers are told that it

is a painful way to attain a supernatural happiness. But the Ur-Fascist hero aspires to death, hailed as the finest reward for a heroic life. The Ur-Fascist hero is impatient to die. In his impatience, it should be noted, he usually manages to make others die in his place.

12. Since both permanent war and heroism are difficult games to play, the Ur-Fascist transfers his will to power onto sexual questions. This is the origin of *machismo* (which implies contempt for women and an intolerant condemnation of nonconformist sexual habits, from chastity to homosexuality). Since sex is also a difficult game to play, the Ur-Fascist hero plays with weapons, which are his ersatz penis: his war games are due to a permanent state of penis envy.

13. Ur-Fascism is based on 'qualitative populism.' In a democracy the citizens enjoy individual rights, but as a whole the citizens have a political impact only from a quantitative point of view (the decisions of the majority are followed). For Ur-Fascists individuals have no rights, and the 'people'

is conceived of as a monolithic entity that expresses the 'common will.' Since no quantity of human beings can possess a common will, the leader claims to be their interpreter. Having lost their power to delegate, the citizens do not act, they are only called upon, *pars pro toto*, to play their role as the people. The people is thus merely a theatrical pretence. For a good example of qualitative populism, we no longer need Piazza Venezia or the stadium in Nuremberg. In our future there looms *qualitative TV* or *Internet populism*, in which the emotional response of a selected group of citizens can be presented and accepted as the 'voice of the people.' As a result of its qualitative populism, Ur-Fascism *has to oppose 'rotten' parliamentary governments*. One of the first things Mussolini said in the Italian parliament was, 'I could have transformed this grey and sordid chamber into a bivouac for my soldiers.' As a matter of fact, he immediately found a better billet for his soldiery, but shortly after that he dissolved the parliament. Every time a politician casts doubt on the legitimacy of a parliament because it no longer represents the 'voice of the people,' there is a suspicion of Ur-Fascism.

14. Ur-Fascism uses newspeak. 'Newspeak' was invented by Orwell in *1984*, as the official language of Ingsoc, the English Socialist movement, but elements of Ur-Fascism are common to different forms of dictatorship. All the Nazi and Fascist scholastic texts were based on poor vocabulary and elementary syntax, the aim being to limit the instruments available to complex and critical reasoning. But we must be prepared to identify other types of newspeak, even when they take the innocent form of a popular talk show.

Now that I have listed the possible characteristics of Ur-Fascism, let me come to a conclusion. On the morning of 27 July 1943 I learned from a radio news broadcast that Fascism had collapsed and Mussolini had been arrested. My mother sent me to buy a newspaper. I went to the nearest newsstand and saw that there were newspapers, but the names were different. Moreover, after a quick glance at the headlines, I realised that every newspaper said something different. I bought one at random and read the message printed on the front page, signed by five or six political parties, like Democrazia Cristiana, Partito Comunista, Partito Socialista, Partito d'Azione, and Partito Liberale. Until that moment I had believed that there was only one party in every country, and that in Italy there was only the National Fascist Party. I was discovering that in my country there could be many different parties at the same time. What's more, since I was a smart kid I realised right away that all those parties could not have emerged overnight. Thus I understood that they had already existed as clandestine organisations.

The message celebrated the end of the dictatorship and the return of freedom: freedom of speech, of the press, of political association. My God, I had never read words like 'freedom' or 'dictatorship' in all my life. By virtue of these words I was reborn as a free Western man.

We must make sure that the sense of these words is not forgotten again. Ur-Fascism is still around us, sometimes in civilian clothes. It would be so easy for us if someone would look out onto the world's stage and say: 'I want to reopen Auschwitz, I want the Blackshirts to march through the streets of Italy once more!'

Alas, life is not so simple. Ur-Fascism can still return in the most innocent of guises. Our duty is to unmask it and to point the finger at each of its new forms – every day, in every part of the world. Once more I yield the floor to Roosevelt: 'I dare to say that if American democracy ceased to progress as a living force, seeking night and day by peaceful means to improve the condition of our citizens, the power of Fascism would grow in our country' (4 November 1938). Freedom and liberation are never-ending tasks. Let this be our motto: 'Do not forget.'

And now I should like to close with a poem by Franco Fortini:

> *On the parapet of the bridge*
> *The heads of hanged men*
> *In the water of the fountain*
> *The drool of hanged men*
>
> *On the cobbles of the market*
> *The fingernails of men shot down*
> *On the dry grass of the meadow*
> *The teeth of men shot down*
>
> *Bite the air bite the stones*
> *Our flesh is the flesh of men no more*

Bite the air bite the stones
Our hearts are the hearts of men no more.

But we have read the dead men's eyes
And the world's freedom is the gift we bring
While the coming justice is close
Clenched in the hands of the dead.

Translated by Alastair McEwen

Censorship and Silence

Those of you who are younger may think that *veline* are pretty girls who dance about on television shows, and that a *casino* is a chaotic mess.[1] Anyone of my generation knows that the word *casino* used to mean 'brothel' and only later, by connotation, did it come to mean 'somewhere chaotic,' so that it lost its initial meaning, and today anyone, perhaps even a bishop, uses it to indicate disorder. Likewise, once upon a time a bordello was a brothel, but my grandmother, a woman of the most upright morals, used to say, 'Don't make a bordello,' meaning 'Don't make too much racket'; the word had completely lost its original meaning. The younger ones among

---

[1] *Translator's note:* The word *casino* in Italian is in effect two words, with two pronunciations – a *casinò*, with the accent on the final syllable, is the same as the English casino, or gambling house; but here we are concerned with the other word *casino*, pronounced, confusingly, with the stress on the penultimate syllable in exactly the same way as the English word.

you may not know that, during the Fascist regime, *veline* were sheets of paper that the government department responsible for controlling culture (called the Ministry of Popular Culture, shortened to MinCulPop – they didn't have sufficient sense of humour to avoid such an ambiguous-sounding name) sent to the newspapers. These sheets of thin copy paper told the newspapers what they had to keep quiet about and what they had to print. The *velina*, in journalistic jargon, therefore came to symbolise censorship, the inducement to conceal, to make information disappear.[2]

The *veline* that we know today – the television showgirls – are, however, the exact opposite: they are, as we all know, the celebration of

---

[2]Now that we have established what *veline* originally were, I can explain how the word came to take on its present meaning. When Antonio Ricci started the television entertainment show *Striscia la notizia* in the 1990s, he wanted some girls, usually appearing on roller-skates, to bring messages for the two presenters, and he called them *veline*. But the choice is very significant; it means that when Ricci created *Striscia la notizia,* the fact that he could make a joke out of the word *veline* indicated there was still an audience that remembered and knew what the *veline* sent out by the MinCulPop were. If no one knows this today, it is another reflection that can be made on 'noise,' on the superimposition of information: in the space of two decades one notion is cancelled out because it has been taken over by the obsessive use of another.

outward appearance, visibility, indeed of fame achieved through pure visibility, where appearance signifies excellence – even that kind of appearance that would once have been considered unseemly.

We find ourselves with two forms of *velina*, which I would like to compare with two forms of censorship. The first is censorship through silence; the second is censorship through noise; I use the word *velina*, therefore, as a symbol of the television event, the show, entertainment, news coverage, and so on.

Fascism had understood (as dictators generally do) that deviant behaviour is encouraged by the fact that the media give it coverage. For example, the *veline* used to say 'Don't write about suicide' because the mere mention of suicide might inspire someone to commit suicide a few days later. This is absolutely correct – we shouldn't assume all that went through the minds of the Fascist hierarchy was wrong – and it is quite true that we know about events of national significance that have occurred only because the media have talked about them. For example, the student protests of 1977 and 1989: they were short-lived events that sought to repeat the protests of 1968 only because the newspapers had begun saying '1968 is about to return.' Anyone involved in those events knows perfectly well that they were created by the press, in the same way that the press generates revenge attacks, suicides, classroom shootings – news about one school shooting provokes other school shootings, and a great many Romanians have probably been encouraged to rape old ladies because the newspapers told them it is the exclusive speciality of immigrants and is extremely easy to commit: all you have to do is loiter in any pedestrian passage, near a railway station, and so forth.

If the old-style *velina* used to say, 'To avoid causing behaviour considered to be deviant, don't talk about it,' the *velina* culture of today says, 'To avoid talking about deviant behaviour, talk a great deal about other things.' I have always taken the view that if, by some chance, I discovered that tomorrow's newspapers were going to take up some wrong I had committed that would cause me serious harm, the first thing I'd do would be plant a bomb outside the local police headquarters or railway station. The next day the newspaper front pages would be full of it and my personal misdemeanour would end up as a small inside story. And who knows how many real bombs have been planted to make other front-page stories disappear. The example of the bomb is sonically appropriate, as it is an example of a great noise that silences everything else.

Noise becomes a cover. I would say that the ideology of this censorship through noise can be expressed, with apologies to Wittgenstein, by saying, 'Whereof one cannot speak, thereof one must talk a great deal.' The flagship *TG1* news programme on Italian state television, for example, is a master of this technique, full of news items about calves born with two heads and bags snatched by petty thieves – in other words, the sort of minor stories papers used to put low on an inside page – which now serve to fill up three-quarters of an hour of information, to ensure we don't notice other news stories they ought to have covered have not been covered. Several months ago, the press controlled by Berlusconi, in order to undermine the authority of a magistrate who criticised the premier, followed him for days, reporting that he sat smoking on a bench, went to the barber, and wore turquoise socks. To make a noise, you don't have to invent stories. All you have to do is report a story that is real but irrelevant, yet creates a hint of suspicion by the simple fact that it has been reported. It is true and irrelevant that the magistrate wears turquoise socks, but the fact it has been reported creates a suggestion of something not quite confessed, leaving a mark, an impression. Nothing is more difficult to dispose of than an irrelevant but true story.

The error made by *La Repubblica* in its campaign against Berlusconi was to give too much coverage to a relevant story (the party at Noemi's house).[3] If, instead, it had reported something like this – 'Berlusconi went into Piazza Navona yesterday morning, met his cousin, and they had a beer together . . . how curious' – it would have triggered such a series of insinuations, suspicions, and embarrassments that the premier would have resigned long ago. In short, a fact that is too relevant can be challenged, whereas an accusation that is not an accusation cannot be challenged.

At the age of ten I was stopped in the doorway of a bar by a lady who said, 'I'll give you one lira if you write a letter for me – I've hurt

---

[3]*Translator's note:* Silvio Berlusconi appeared as a guest at a girl's eighteenth-birthday party in April 2009, prompting his wife to file for divorce.

my hand.' Being a decent child I replied that I
didn't want any money and would do it simply
as a favour, but the lady insisted on buying me an
ice cream. I wrote the letter for her and explained
what had happened when I got home. 'Good
Lord,' said my mother, 'they've made you write
an anonymous letter. Heaven knows what will
happen to us when they find out!' 'Look,' I
explained, 'there's nothing terrible in that letter.'
In fact, it was addressed to a wealthy business-
man, whom I also knew (he had a shop in the
city centre) and it said, 'It has come to our attention that you intend to ask for the hand of
Signorina X in marriage. We wish to inform you
that Signorina X is from a respectable and pros-
perous family and is highly regarded throughout
the city.' Now, you don't usually see an anonymous letter that praises the subject of the letter
rather than damning her. But what was the purpose of that anonymous letter? Since the lady
who recruited me clearly had no grounds for
saying anything else, she wanted at least to create unease. The recipient would have wondered,
'Why should they send me such a letter? What
does "highly regarded throughout the city"
actually mean?' I believe the wealthy business-
man would have decided in the end to postpone

the idea of marriage for fear of setting up home with someone so gossiped about.

This form of noise doesn't even require that the transmitted messages be of any particular interest, since one message adds to another, and together they create noise. Noise can sometimes take the form of superfluous excess. A few months ago there was a fine article by Berselli in *L'Espresso* magazine, saying, Do you realize that advertising no longer has any effect on us? No one can prove that one soap powder is better than another (in fact they are all the same), so for the past fifty years the only method anyone has come up with shows us housewives who refuse the offer of two packets in exchange for their own brand, or grandmothers who tell us that this recalcitrant stain will disappear if we use the right powder. Soap companies therefore carry out an intensive and relentless campaign, consisting of the same message, which everyone knows by heart, so that it becomes proverbial: 'Omo washes whiter than white,' and so on. Its purpose is twofold: partly to repeat the brand name (in certain cases it becomes a successful strategy: if I have to go into a supermarket and ask for soap powder, I will ask for Tide or Omo because I have known these names for the past fifty years), and partly to prevent anyone from realising that no epideictic discussion can be made about soap powder – either for or against. And the same happens with other forms of advertising: Berselli observes that in every mobile phone advert, none of us actually understand what the characters are saying. But there's no need to understand what they say – it is the great noise that sells cell phones. I think it is most probable that companies have jointly agreed to stop promoting their own particular brands and to carry out general publicity, to spread the mobile telephone culture. If you buy Nokia instead of Samsung, you will be persuaded by other factors, but not by advertising. In fact the main function of the publicity noise is to remind you of the advertising sketch, not the product. Try to think of the most pleasant, the most enjoyable piece of advertising – some are even quite funny – and to remember which product it relates to. It is very rare that you manage to remember the name of the product to which that advertisement refers: the child who mispronounces 'Simmenthal,' or perhaps 'No Martini, no party' or 'Ramazzotti is always good for you.' In all other cases the noise compensates for the fact that there is no way to demonstrate the excellence of the product.

The Internet, of course, generates, with no intention to censor, the greatest noise that yields no information. Or rather: first, you receive information, but you don't know whether it is reliable; second, you try searching for information on the Internet: only we academics and researchers, after ten minutes' work, can begin to select the information we want. Most other users are stuck on blogs, or on a porn site, and so forth, without surfing too far, because surfing isn't going to help them find reliable information.

Looking further at cases of noise that do not presuppose any intention to censure, but nevertheless tend toward censorship, we should also mention the newspaper with sixty-four pages. Sixty-four pages are too many to give real prominence to the most essential information. Here again, some of you will say, 'But I buy a newspaper to find the news that interests me.' Certainly, but those who do that are an elite who know how to deal with information – and there must be some good explanation for the frightening drop in the number of newspapers being sold and read. Young people no longer read newspapers. It is easier to find the *La Repubblica* or *Corriere della Sera* sites on the Internet – there, at least, it is all on one screen – or to read the free sheets at the train station, where the news is set out on two pages.

Therefore, as a result of noise, we have a deliberate censorship – this is what is happening in the world of television, in creating political scandals, and so forth – and we have an involuntary but fatal censorship whereby, for reasons that are entirely legitimate in themselves (such as advertising revenue, product sales, and so forth), an excess of information is transformed into noise. This (and here I am moving from communications to ethics) has also created a psychology and morality of noise. Look at that idiot walking along the street, wearing his iPod headphones; he cannot spend an hour on the train reading a newspaper or looking at the countryside, but has to go straight to his mobile phone during the first part of the journey to say 'I've just left' and on the second part of the journey to say 'I'm just arriving.' There are people now who cannot live away from noise. And it is for this reason that restaurants, already noisy places, offer extra noise from a television screen – sometimes two – and music; and if you ask for them to be switched off, people stare at you as if you're mad. This great need for noise is like a drug; it is a way to avoid focusing on what is really important. *Redi in interiorem hominem:* yes, in the end, the example of Saint Augustine could still provide a good ideal for the world of politics and television.

It is in silence alone that the only truly powerful means of information becomes effective – word of mouth. All people, even when they are oppressed by the most censorious tyrants, have been able to find out all that is going on in the world through popular word of mouth. Publishers know that books do not become bestsellers through publicity or reviews but by what the French call *bouche à oreille* and the Italians call *passaparola* – books achieve success through word of mouth. In losing the condition of silence, we lose the possibility of hearing what other people are saying, which is the only basic and reliable means of communication.

And that is why, in conclusion, I would say that one of the ethical problems we face today is how to return to silence. And one of the semiotic problems we might consider is the closer study of the function of silence in various aspects of communication, to examine a semiotics of silence: it may be a semiotics of reticence, a semiotics of silence in theatre, a semiotics of silence in politics, a semiotics of silence in political debate – in other words, the long pause, silence as creation of suspense, silence as threat, silence as agreement, silence as denial, silence in music. Look how many subjects there are to study concerning the semiotics of silence. I invite you to consider, therefore, not words but silence.

Translated by Richard Dixon

We Are European

In 1678 and 1679, Nijmegen hosted delegates from dozens of European countries and city states whose aim was to resolve a series of wars that had devastated our continent. The resulting Treaties of Nijmegen ended a variety of interrelated wars that had raged until then between France, the Netherlands, Spain, Brandenburg, Sweden, Denmark, the Prince-Bishopric of Münster and the Holy Roman Empire. Even though the treaties were subsequently disregarded, this effort was (after the horrors of the Thirty Years' War) the first example of an attempt to establish peace through dialogue and negotiations. This could therefore be seen as one of the first examples of European cooperation and accord and can be said to be a key event in European history.

Over two hundred and fifty years went by between those treaties and 1945, but we can say that the utopia born in Nijmegen came of age at the end of the Second World War.

It is a source of constant congratulation for people of my generation (whereas our children and grandchildren find it obvious) that today it is inconceivable (ridiculous, even) to think of a possible war between France and Germany, Italy and Great Britain, Spain and the Low Countries. Young people – if they are not history students – find it hard to comprehend that such conflicts have been the norm for the last two thousand years. Sometimes even older people are not consciously aware of this, except perhaps when they feel a thrill on crossing European frontiers without a passport and without having to change money. But it's worth remembering that not only our distant ancestors but also our fathers were accustomed to crossing those same frontiers with guns in their hands.

From 1945 onward, almost without realising it, Europeans began to feel they belonged not only to the same continent but also to the same community, despite the many inevitable linguistic and cultural differences. I am not a naive idealist and I am well aware that if Europeans are no longer shooting at one another, there are nonetheless many forms of no less violent contention that often divide our countries – the current financial crisis, for example, is not producing a new sense of brotherhood so much as an atmosphere of mutual distrust. The sense of a European identity may neither look the same to nor seem obvious to all the citizens of the various nations, but at least among the more responsible citizens, and especially among the more cultured young people (for example, students on the Erasmus programme who live together with their fellows from other countries and who often marry each another, thereupon raising a new, bilingual generation), the idea of being European is ever more widespread.

Perhaps we do not feel European enough when we travel in Europe and are still disturbed by our neighbours' different customs, but a visit to another continent suffices to make us realise that, even if we like these distant countries, when we meet another European abroad we get the feeling that we are back home talking with someone we understand. Suddenly, we catch a whiff of something familiar and so an Italian may feel more at ease with a Norwegian than with an American.

There are countless reasons why a French person may think differently from a German, but both have been formed by a series of shared experiences, from wealth gained through disputes over work rather than an individualistic ethic of success, to the old pride in and the subsequent failure of colonialism, not to mention the experience of dreadful dictatorships (and not only have we experienced those but by now we are also able to recognise the warning signs). We have been vaccinated by the many wars in our countries: sometimes I think that if two aeroplanes had crashed into Notre-Dame or Big Ben, we would certainly have been devastated, but without the feelings of inexplicable bewilderment, desperate incredulity and depression that struck Americans on being attacked by an enemy in their own country for the first time in their history. Our tragedies have made us wise and ruthless, better prepared to deal with horror. We seek peace because we have known too many wars.

But we must be realistic and recognise that, despite all this, wars, hatred and intolerance persist within Europe's borders. We must be aware that new forms of conflict obsess us, even when we do not perceive them in all their magnitude and importance.

Within our frontiers we are still involved in a (sometimes hidden) form of warfare with people who live in Europe but who we (or at least many of our fellow countrymen) continue to think of as 'non-EU nationals'. [. . .]

The problem that now concerns a reconciled Europe, one which can optimistically celebrate the triumph of the spirit of the Nijmegen treaties, is the need to sign a new virtual treaty against intolerance.

The struggle against our intolerance does not only regard so-called 'non-EU nationals'. It is a form of illusion to consider the new cases of anti-Semitism as a marginal sickness that affects only a lunatic fringe. Recent episodes tell us that the spectre of this obsession is still among us.

Today in Nijmegen, as we celebrate that first dream of European peace, we must declare war on racism. If we are unable to defeat this eternal adversary we will always be at war, even if we have laid down our arms – for there are still many weapons in circulation, as was demonstrated by the massacre on the Norwegian island of Utøya or by the slaughter in the Jewish school in France. [. . .]

Nonetheless, the war on intolerance has its limits. Fighting against our own intolerance does not mean having to accept every world view or make ethical relativism the new European religion. While we educate our fellow citizens and

especially our children to open-minded tolerance, we should also recognise that there are
customs, ideas and behaviours that are – and
must remain – intolerable to us. Some values
typical of the European world view represent a
heritage we must not relinquish. To decide on
and recognise those things that, even within a
tolerant world view, remain intolerable is the
kind of frontier that Europeans are called upon
to draw up every day, with a sense of equity
and the constant exercise of that virtue which,
from Aristotle onwards, philosophers have called
prudence.

From a philosophical standpoint, prudence
does not signify a reluctance to take risks, nor
does it coincide with cowardice. In the classical
meaning of *phronesis*, prudence is the ability to
control and discipline oneself through the use of
reason, and as such it has been considered one of
the four cardinal virtues and is often associated
with wisdom and intuition, the capacity to
judge between good and bad actions, not only in
a general sense, but with regard to opportune
action at a given time and place.

It must be possible, in our collective war on
intolerance, to always distinguish between the
tolerable and the intolerable. It must be possible

to decide how to accept a new plurality of values and customs without giving up the best of our European heritage. I am not here today to propose solutions to the fundamental problem of a new European peace, but to affirm that only by facing the challenge of this ever-present war will we have a peaceful future.

What we need to do now is sign a new treaty of Nijmegen.

Translated by Alastair McEwen

THE LEOPARD

The leopard is one of Harvill's historic colophons and an imprimatur of the highest quality literature from around the world.

When The Harvill Press was founded in 1946 by former Foreign Office colleagues Manya Harari and Marjorie Villiers (hence Har-vill), it was with the express intention of rebuilding cultural bridges after the Second World War. As their first catalogue set out: 'The editors believe that by producing translations of important books they are helping to overcome the barriers, which at present are still big, to close interchange of ideas between people who are divided by frontiers.' The press went on to publish from many different languages, with highlights including Giuseppe Tomasi di Lampedusa's *The Leopard*, Boris Pasternak's *Doctor Zhivago*, José Saramago's *Blindness*, W. G. Sebald's *The Rings of Saturn*, Henning Mankell's *Faceless Killers* and Haruki Murakami's *Norwegian Wood*.

In 2005 The Harvill Press joined with Secker & Warburg, a publisher with its own illustrious history of publishing international writers. In 2020, Harvill Secker reintroduced the leopard to launch a new translated series celebrating some of the finest and most exciting voices of the twenty-first century.

Umberto Eco (1932–2016) wrote fiction, literary criticism and philosophy. His first novel, *The Name of the Rose*, was a major international bestseller. His other works include *Foucault's Pendulum*, *The Island of the Day Before*, *Baudolino*, *The Mysterious Flame of Queen Loana*, *The Prague Cemetery* and *Numero Zero* along with many brilliant collections of essays.